I0191880

Edmund Head

Ballads and Other Poems

Original and translated

Edmund Head

Ballads and Other Poems
Original and translated

ISBN/EAN: 9783744795425

Printed in Europe, USA, Canada, Australia, Japan

Cover: Foto ©Thomas Meinert / pixelio.de

More available books at **www.hansebooks.com**

BALLADS AND OTHER POEMS.

ORIGINAL AND TRANSLATED.

BY THE LATE

RIGHT HON. SIR EDMUND HEAD, BART., K.C.B.

SMITH, ELDER AND CO., LONDON.
1868.

CONTENTS.

———◦◦———

PREFACE.

——◆◇◆——

SIR EDMUND HEAD, shortly before his death, had collected these poems and translations (which had appeared from time to time in *Fraser's Magazine*) with a view to their being reprinted for private distribution amongst his friends. Those to whom the disposal of them has devolved have thought it better to republish them than to reprint them privately, because the circle of his friends and of those who take a friendly interest in dwelling upon all that he was and all that he did, is a very wide circle, and it would be difficult perhaps for any one to know where it ends, so as to include in a private distribution all whom he would himself have wished to be included, and all to whom any record of his mind, even in its lighter and more excursive operations, or any traces of his steps on earth, will have a value. It is for this memorial value that they are thus preserved; not certainly as representing more than one or two of the bye-paths into which he occasionally betook himself when the main business and purposes of his life permitted : for—though loving literature with an exceeding love, and knowing the literature of divers times and countries with the knowledge to which only love can lead, and with an extent of knowledge to which few, even through love, have found their way—he gave his life, after his first youth, to the public service at home and abroad, and such productions as these were merely the fruits of occasional retirement into literature when resting from public labours.

BALLADS AND OTHER POEMS.

FREE TRANSLATION OF THE LAST ELEGY OF PROPERTIUS.

[B. v., EL. 11.]

[Supposed to be addressed by Cornelia, a Roman matron, to her
husband and children after her death. Certain lines relating
to mythology, and a few others, are omitted.]

I.

VEX not the grave with tears : its shadows deep
 Repulse the mourner and exclude the day :
The bourne is passed : cease, Paulus, cease to weep ;
 A gate of adamant hath barr'd the way.

I

II.

Prayer dies in echoes 'mid these gloomy bowers,
　And floats in vain round sullen Pluto's ear :
Prayer moves the Gods above : th' infernal powers
　Nor list the suppliant voice, nor heed the tear.

III.

Such were the truths taught by the trumpet's blare,
　When o'er my bier curl'd up the funeral flame ;
What booted then our troth, or lineage fair,
　Or those bright pledges which have graced our name ?

IV.

Could I thus 'scape from Fate's unbending laws ?
　No ! five small fingers now may lift my dust.
All young and spotless let me plead my cause
　To Æacus and Minos—stern, yet just.

V.

If any maid could vaunt her sires in Rome,
　Ancestral fame was mine on either side ;
For Spain and Carthage deck'd with spoils the home
　Where Scipio's blood was match'd with Libo's pride.

VI.

A girl, dear Paulus, on our wedding day
 I wreath'd the bridal fillet in my hair :
And soon, too soon, in death thus snatch'd away,
 No second name upon my tomb I bear.

VII.

Shades of our fathers ! ye, whose titles tell
 Of Afric shorn of empire at your feet ;
And how the braggart race of Perseus fell—
 Achilles' sons hurl'd from Achilles' seat—

VIII.

Stand forth, and witness that no sland'rer's breath
 E'er tainted on the Censor's roll my name ;
Between the bridal torch and torch of death
 We liv'd and lov'd in wedded faith the same.

IX.

It needed not a judge or law to guide
 One, in whose veins the blood of all her race
Swell'd with the instinct of a conscious pride,
 And bade maintain a Roman matron's place.

X.

I shrink from none.   If ancient tales be true,
  When Vesta's fire was quench'd, Emilia's hand
Her linen garment o'er the ashes threw,
  And show'd beneath its folds the kindled brand.

XI.

We know how Claudia's slender girdle mov'd
  The Mighty Mother's ship : their vestal pride
Will hail the faith in steadfast wedlock prov'd,
  And greet Cornelia seated at their side.

XII.

Thou too, Scribonia, gentle mother, say,
  Now thou art weeping o'er thy daughter's tomb,
What is there in my course to wish away,
  Save that I met in death an early doom ?

XIII.

"Tis something for a mother, when she dies,
  To leave no barren hearth, no desert home ;
I joy to think that sons have clos'd my eyes
  Who live to bear their ancient name in Rome.

XIV.

My daughter ! let the world retrace in thee
  The even tenour of thy mother's life :
Like me prolong thy line, and die like me,
  Firm in thy plighted troth, but once a wife.

XV.

A woman's brighter triumph is attain'd
  When blame no more can wound nor flatt'ry move,
When praise from all, unbrib'd and unrestrain'd,
  Meets o'er her bier the tears of those who love.

XVI.

Still, Paulus, in my ashes lives one care ;
  Our children of their mother are bereft :
The household charge we both were wont to share
  In undivided weight on thee is left.

XVII.

Affection's duty now devolves on thee :
  Oh ! let them not a mother's fondness miss,
But when they clasp thy neck or climb thy knee,
  Add to their sire's caress a mother's kiss.

XVIII.

Be careful, if thou e'er for me shalt weep,
  That they may never mark the tears thus shed ;
Let it suffice thyself to mourn in sleep
  The wife whose spirit hovers o'er thy bed ;

XIX.

Or in thy chamber, if thou wilt, aloud
  Address that wife as if she could reply :
Dim not our children's joys with sorrow's cloud,
  But dry the tear, and check the rising sigh.

XX.

You too, my children, at your father's side,
  In after years a step-dame if you see,
Let no rash word offend her jealous pride,
  Nor indiscreetly wound by praising me.

XXI.

Obey his will in all : and should he bear
  In widow'd solitude the woes of age,
Let it be yours to prop his steps with care,
  And with your gentle love those woes assuage.

XXII.

I lost no child : 'twas mine in death to see
   Their faces cluster'd round : nor should I grieve
If but the span of life cut off from me
   Could swell the years in store for those I leave.

XXIII.

My cause is pleaded and my tale is told :
   Pronounce me worthy of the meed I claim,
And give me, where my fathers sleep of old,
   Such honour as befits Cornelia's house and name.

Bodas hacian en Francia
Allá dentro de Paris, etc.

GRIMM, *Silva de Romances*, p. 249.

I.

THE wedding is in Paris,
   Within the realm of France.
How well the Lady Beatrice
   Leads off the wedding dance!
And how the Count Don Martin
   Stands there that dance to see—
" Or gaze ye on the dance, Sir Count,
   " Or gaze ye thus on me?"

II.

" The dance ! fair maid ? 'tis not the dance,

  " That thus can charm mine eye ;

" I gaze upon thy face and form,

  " And, as I gaze, I sigh."

" And is it so, Sir Count ? " she says—

  " Then take me for your bride,

" Or here to-night, a wedded wife,

  " I shall grace a dotard's side."

[B. iv., EL. iii.]

Letter from a wife to her husband with the army in the East.

———••◦•———

I.

My own Lycotas ! let this scroll from me
   Tell Arethusa's love ; though at each line
I pause, and doubt if one I never see,
   So long, so often, absent, can be mine.

II.

Think, when thou see'st the page defac'd and blurr'd,
   Each blot a tear affection bade me shed ;
Think each imperfect stroke and faulty word
   Trac'd by a hand which quivers all but dead.

III.

O'er Bactria's sands twice hast thou march'd in war;
    Hast seen on barbed steed the Tartar ride—
The frozen Getæ—Britain's painted car—
    And the dark Indian by the Eastern tide.

IV.

Is such a husband's faith? And did I buy
    No other love than this, when as thy bride,
A girl with blushing cheek and downcast eye,
    I heard thee plead, and vail'd my maiden pride?

V.

Some fun'ral pyre our bridal torch had lit;
    They set awry the fillet in my hair,
And sprinkled waters from the Stygian pit:
    All evil omens—not the gods—were there.

VI.

Yes! everywhere my vows in vain are paid:
    Thy cloak I weave this fourth revolving year,
And curse whoe'er first fram'd a palisade
    Or bade the trumpet sound its note of fear.

VII.

Doth the spear gall those gentle hands of thine,
    Or corslet chafe those arms and shoulders fair?
I care not—so they round no other twine,
    And wanton lips imprint no kisses there.

VIII.

Men tell me that the glow of youthful sheen
    No longer on thy pallid face they see:
I only pray such changes in thy mien
    May mark the fond regret thou feel'st for me.

IX.

When twilight wanes and sinks in bitter night,
    I kiss thy scatter'd arms, and restless lie
And toss, complaining till the tardy light
    Hath wak'd the birds that sing of morning nigh.

X.

The scarlet fleece, when winter evenings close,
    I wind on shuttles for thy warlike weeds;
Or study in what course Araxes flows,
    And how the Parthians press their hardy steeds.

XI.

I turn the map and struggle hard to learn
    Where God hath plac'd the land and where the sea ;
What climes are stiff with frost, what summers burn,
    And guess what wind may waft thee home to me.

XII.

One sister sits beside me, pale with cares :
    My old nurse wonders at thy lengthen'd stay,
And totters to and fro, and chides, and swears
    'Tis only winter keeps thee still away.

XIII.

In barbarous freedom glad Hippolyté
    Could bare her breast, and bind with steel her brow :
As fain in tent and field I'd follow thee
    If Roman wives might tend the camp-fire now.

XIV.

Not Scythia's icy crags nor frozen streams
    Should bar my way : Love ev'ry heart doth tame ;
But in a wife who waits her lord, it seems,
    'Tis Venus' self who fans the living flame.

XV.

" Why do I wear this purple robe ? " I ask ;
  " Why let my widow'd hand with jewels shine ? "
The house is silent all : her lonely task
  One maiden plies in these proud halls of thine.

XVI.

I like to hear our little Glaucis whine
  As if for thee : she only shares my bed.
I load with flow'rs and vervain every shrine,
  And on the hearth the crackling incense shed.

XVII.

It matters not what omens, bad or good,
  The hooting owl or sputt'ring lamp may show :
In fear or thankfulness a victim's blood
  By the priest's ready knife is sure to flow.

XVIII.

Ah ! seek not out some chief in battle-fray
  Whose perfum'd scarf may of thy prowess tell :
Nor, wild for honour, dare upon that day
  To head the storm of Bactria's citadel—

XIX.

That day when barb'rous slings with whizzing sound
    Pour on our host their bullets' deadly rain,
And as each Parthian wheels his courser round,
    The twanging bowstring tells a Roman slain.

XX.

Thy lance erect, borne through triumphant Rome,
    Behind the victor's car I pray to see—
If only well assur'd thou bringest home
    A faith unstain'd, a heart still true to me.

XXI.

Then to the Capenian Gate I'll joyous go,
    And thank the gods for honour and for life :
I'll hang thy trophied arms, and write below—
    " These for her husband from a grateful wife."

BALLAD:

FOUNDED ON A STORY GIVEN IN CONDÉ'S *Historia de los Arabes en España,* vol. ii. p. 262.

[This story is curious as illustrating the feelings of Western chivalry which prevailed on both sides in these frontier contests between the Spaniards and the Moors, notwithstanding the difference of religion. The adoption by the kings of Granada of a sort of coat of arms, as seen in the decorations of the Alhambra, points to the same *inter-penetration* of the notions of the two races thus in contact.]

I.

FROM Antequera's late-won walls
At the close of a summer's day,
Narvaez sent ten chosen men
To drive a Moorish prey.

II.

Right March-men all, with batter'd helms
  And true Toledo blades,
They talk'd as they rode of Granada's wealth
  And her dark ey'd Moorish maids;

III.

How the foray burst from each well-known pass,
  And scar'd the frontier bands :
How they drove the kine and swept the slaves
  From the Vega's smoking lands;

IV.

Or how they laugh'd from the mountain brow
  To see for the rescue late,
The glitt'ring line of gennet and plume
  Stream forth from Elvira's gate;

V.

And now they had hemm'd Granada in,
  And hoped, on the banks of Xenil,
By our Lady's grace to plant in short space
  The banner and cross of Castile.

VI.

They linger'd on till night should dim
  The Moorish warder's eye,
When a hoof-tramp borne upon the breeze
  Bespoke a horseman nigh.

VII.

A gallant rode deep sunk in thought ;
  He woke as from a trance,
Too late to grasp his scimitar,
  And too late to poise his lance,

VIII.

When they seiz'd his rein, and search'd—it seem'd
  That the barb and his rider's air,
With his jewelled vest and baldric of gold,
  Must promise a ransom fair :

IX.

So to Antequera they led him back,
  And when Narvaez came,
He greeted the youth with courtesy,
  And crav'd his rank and name.

X.

In silent thought the captive stood
 As though his senses slept;
And when the question struck his ear
 He started, gaz'd, and wept.

XI.

The Spaniard check'd a sneer, but look'd
 With wonder on his mood,
For his practis'd eye could not misken
 The marks of gentle blood.

XII.

The Moor replied at length—" For myself
 " I am known by my own good sword,
" But better far for my father's fame,
 " Who is rocky Ronda's Lord."

XIII.

" I question not the race or name
 " Which thy words and bearing speak ;
" I marvel though that a woman's tears
 " Should stain a warrior's cheek."

XIV.

" I weep not thus, Sir Count," he said,
  " The chance of war to prove :
" I weep to fail in the plighted word
  " I had given my Lady-love :

XV.

" For a twelvemonth past to that maiden fair
  " Hath my tale of love been told :
" I had vow'd to bear her forth to-night
  " From Archidona's hold."

XVI.

Narvaez paus'd—" Though an infidel,
  " Thou com'st of a knightly strain—
" Wilt thou visit thy love on the word of a knight
  " To render thyself again ? "

XVII.

" Right gladly I will ! "—He mounted his barb,
  And spurr'd him down from the tower,
And soon he sat by his true-love's side
  Within her maiden bower.

XVIII.

" I know thee not again," she said,
 " With that unwonted sigh ;
 " And where is the glance of eager joy
 " That flash'd in the lover's eye ? "

XIX.

·" Can I smile when I come as a captive thrall,
 " Releas'd on my plighted word ?
 " Can I carry thee forth to share my lot
 " As the slave of a Christian Lord ? "

XX.

The maiden rose ; she took her veil,
 And as she donn'd it, said—
 " I teach thee to know, in weal or woe,
 " The truth of a Moorish maid.

XXI.

" It may be that this casket's gems
 " Their greedy souls will move ;
 " It may be e'en the infidel
 " Will pity constant love.

XXII.

" But come what may, I vow'd to-night
　　" To fly from my father's side ;
" A slave or free, 'tis one to me—
　　" I still shall be thy bride."

XXIII.

He strove in vain : at his gennet's croup
　　That lady left her bower ;
And as morning dawn'd the Moor and his bride
　　Were in Antequera's tower.

XXIV.

And old Narvaez wept when he saw
　　The pair before him kneel :
He thought on her he had woo'd and lost
　　Of old, in fair Castile.

XXV.

" I care not for your proffer'd gems :
　　" Sir Knight, ye both are free ;
" This Lady's love and thy word fulfill'd
　　" Shall be ransom for her and thee."

BALLADS FROM THE SPANISH.

THE first of the following poems, like all good ballads, belongs to that class of composition which suggests far more than it narrates. We may assume that the lady whose fate it describes was married against her will to the enemy of her family (see stanza v.), and that the stranger knight is her early love, whom she had been compelled to renounce. The mode in which her husband convicts her, by successive questions, reminds us of a well-known Scotch song of a purely comic character, and it is curious to trace this analogy between two poems of different countries, of which the spirit is so totally different. I allude to the song—the author of which is, I believe, not known—beginning with the following verse :—

> Our gudeman cam hame at e'en,
>   And hame cam he ;
> And there he saw a saddle horse,
>   Where nae horse should be.

> Oh, how cam this horse here?
> How can this be?
> How cam this horse here
> Without the leave o' me?

I am quite aware of the fact that the second ballad cannot be ranked among the highest productions of the class to which it belongs.

> Blanca sois, señora mia,
> Mas que no el rayo del sol, &c.
> > *Primavera de Romances,* vol. ii. p. 52;
> > *Duran,* vol. i. p. 13; *Grimm,* p. 242.

I.

" Thou art fair, thou art fair, O Lady mine,
  " As the beam of morning bright:
" May I rest unarm'd in this bower of thine?
  " May I sleep without fear through the night?

II.

" Seven years, seven years, it hath been the same;
  " These limbs have their harness worn,
" And are blacken'd as if by the furnace-flame,
  " All scath'd by the toils they have borne."

III.

" Thou may'st sleep, Sir Knight, may'st sleep till day ;
    " Unarm'd, thou need'st not fear ;
" To the mountains of Leon the Count is away ;
    " He is gone to chase the deer.

IV.

" My curse go with him ! and ill may he speed !
    " May his hounds die mad, his hawks be slain !
" And dead at the heels of his dark brown steed
    " May I see him dragged to his home again ! "

V.

Whilst thus they are talking, her Lord is there,
    And he calls in scorn and ire—
" Well, what art thou doing, my Lady so fair,
    " Thou child of a traitor sire ? "

VI.

" I was combing my hair, Sir, in sorrowful cheer ;
    " I was combing it all alone,
" Because to the mountains to chase the deer
    " My lord and master had gone."

VII.

" This story, fair lady, a man may doubt ;
 " This story is nought but a lie.
" Say, whose is yon steed that is standing without,
 " And that neigh'd as I came by ? "

VIII.

" That steed is my father's, Sir Count," she said :
 " He hath sent it a gift to thee."
" Whose arms are those in a heap thus laid
 " At thy chamber door I see ? "

IX.

" My brother, Sir Count, he hath sent to thee here
 " Those arms which lie on the floor "——
" Ay, well ! but the spear—say whose is the spear
 " That is leaning against the door ? "

X.

" Take thou that spear—I reck not of life—
 " And slay me where I stand :
" 'T will be but the meed that a perjured wife
 " Hath earn'd at her husband's hand."

"Caballero de lejas tierras," &c.
Primavera de Romances, vol. ii. p. 88.

———◆———

" Thou stranger knight from foreign lands,
   " Whom passing by I see,
" Rein in thy steed and ground thy spear,
   " And speak one word to me.
" Oh ! tell me if perchance abroad
   " My husband thou hast seen ? "
" How should I know unless I learn
   " Thy husband's guise and mien ? "
" My husband is a gentleman,
   " Full young and fair to see,
" Well skilled in chess, and courtly games,
   " And sports of chivalry.
" A Marquis is he, and his arms
   " Grav'd on his sword-hilt bears :
" A surcoat too of rich brocade
   " With crimson lin'd he wears.
" There dangles from his lance's head,
   " And glitters in the sun,
" A pennon fair of Portugal,
   " Which in the lists he won."

" If so it be, O Lady fair,
   " I knew thy husband well :
" In a quarrel at Valencia,
   " That Lord was stabb'd and fell :
" He was struck at play by a Milanese ;
   " And many a knight and dame
" Griev'd for his death, and cherish still
   " Thy gallant husband's name.
" Nay, more than that, men say one maid,
   " The daughter of his host—
" Of Genoa fair by birth she is—
   " Weeps for her lover lost.
" But shouldst thou deign to love again—
   " Is there no hope for me ? "
" No, no, Sir Knight—urge no such suit—
   " A nun I'm doomed to be."
" A nun ! fair dame ?   Thou'rt surely bound
   " To pause awhile," he cried ;
" For 'tis the husband of thy heart
   " Who standeth at thy side ! "

THE DEATH OF OLD KING GORM.

A BALLAD.

THIS ballad is founded on the story told in the Jomsvi-
kingasaga, which, if it be the most striking, is probably
not the most authentic account of the events to which it
relates. Historians seem to think it probable that Knut
was killed in Ireland or in Yorkshire, rather than slain
by his brother Harald in Jutland. Queen Thyra is the
person to whom the Danes owed that work of which we
have again heard within the last few years—the " Dana-
virke." She bore the name of " Thyre Danebod" (Dane's
help) as her son Knut was called " Dana-ast " or " Den-
mark's Darling." In one of the popular songs describing
the erection of the Danavirke, we are told :

> Det var Ord af Dronning Thyre
> Ret kaldt Dannebod
> Kvinden, som ved Danmark's Styre
> Sad med Mandemod.

" The 'Lymfiòrd' is the narrow inlet across the penin-
sula of Jutland, just south of the main channel into the
Baltic ; the western end was formerly closed by a neck of
land from the North Sea, but Mr. Laing says, ' This
neck has, within these fifteen years, been washed away,
and there is now a channel into the Baltic by this new
passage for small craft.' " (Heimskringla, vol. i. p. 378, n.
1884.)   The date of Knut's death was about A. D. 935.

I.

" My brother is slain, and the fight is won !
    " Go now," Earl Harald said ;
" And find me the man that will tell King Gorm,
    " How Knut his son is dead."

II.

He paus'd and look'd on his liegemen all,
    But, I trow, no liegeman spoke ;
He heard but the boom of the heaving tide
    As each crested billow broke.

III.

O'er Lymfiòrd the level sun
    Shed his last rays around,
Where ships and corpses, oars and shields,
    Went drifting up the Sound.

IV.

At length one said : " We know right well
   " That man, Lord Earl, is fey,
" Who shall dare to tell to thy father's face,
   " The deed that was done this day.

V.

" King Gorm hath spoken—who bears that tale,
   " Full sore shall his tidings rue ;
" The death of Knut is the death of the King,
   " And the death of its teller too."

VI.

The Earl hath gone to his mother's bow'r ;
   They have conn'd their counsels o'er,
And when King Gorm at his wine was set
   Earl Harald spoke on the floor :—

VII.

" I saw two falcons fight yestreen,
   " One white—the other grey :
" The grey soar'd high in his pride of place,
   " But the white death-stricken lay."

VIII.

No more he utter'd, and fled from the hall
 As a man for his life doth fly;
But the old King sate with mien unchang'd,
 And drain'd his goblet dry.

IX.

" Now busk ye ! busk ye ! my maidens all,"
 Queen Thyra cried that night,
" For sable hangings must deck my hall
 " In lieu of the scarlet bright."

X.

Again on the morrow King Gorm sat there
 To drink with his liegemen bold;
He look'd on the walls, and he look'd on the Queen,
 And his heart grew chill and cold.

XI.

He rose and rax'd him, while the tears
 Fell fast on his beard like rain—
" Woe ! Denmark, woe ! my hour is come,
 " For Knut my son is slain !"

XII.

" No tongue but thine own hath told the tale,"
 Queen Thyra gently said ;
He leant to the wall—he sunk in his chair—
 And Gorm the King was dead.

THE BRIDAL SONG OF HELEN.

A TRANSLATION FROM THE EIGHTEENTH IDYLL OF
THEOCRITUS.

Ἔν ποκ' ἄρα Σπάρτᾳ ξανθότριχι πὰρ Μενελάῳ, κ. τ. λ.

———•◇•———

WHERE fair-hair'd Menelaus dwelt,
  Great Atreus' younger son,
And Helen to his home was borne,
  Long lov'd, now woo'd and won,
Twelve damsels stood—the hyacinth
  Gleam'd in their braided hair—
First of the land, Laconia's boast,
  A marvel bright and fair—
And wove with twinkling feet the dance,
  And all in concert sung,
As the bridal bower on Helen clos'd,
  And the hall around them rung.

" What ! gentle bridegroom ! gone so soon ?

  " To slumber art thou fled

" In drowsy mood, or tir'd and faint,

  " Or wine hath touch'd thy head.

" Thus early wilt thou sleep—at least

  " Thou shouldst have left the maid,

" That here we girls as comrades all

  " Till morning might have play'd

" Beneath her loving mother's eye ;

  " For well we know for life,

" From year to year, from night to morn,

  " She ever is thy wife.

" With happy omen didst thou come ;

  " Well hath thy wooing sped :

" Thou first among e'en Sparta's chiefs !

  " Jove's daughter shares thy bed ;

" Bless'd were the child that should repeat

  " That mother's form and face,

" No maid that treads the ground of Greece

  " Can vie with Helen's grace.

" We know it—all of equal age,

  " We've bar'd in girlhood's pride

" Our supple limbs in manly sport

  " Along Eurotas' side—

".. Full four times sixty Spartan maids
   " In pastime gather'd here—
" And midst us all—we know it well—
   " There is not Helen's peer.
" The glow of dawn, the burst of spring,
   " The majesty of night—
" They all are fair, but fair as they,
   " She shines in golden light.
" As the tall cypress rears its spire
   " And marks its place afar,
" Some garden's pride—as the fleet steed
   " Adorns the victor's car,
" So Lacedæmon's pride and joy,
   " We see young Helen move,
" And scatter from her blushing brow
   " The rosy light of love.
" No hand like hers can reel the wool,
   " Or weave without a seam,
" With shuttle deft so close a web
   " Cut from the loom's tall beam.
" Ay! and to sweep the sounding lyre
   " And sing high themes like this—
" Broad-breasted Pallas, and the might
   " Of Orthian Artemis—

" No hand, no voice like Helen's is ;
  " Yet in her eyes the while
" All woman's softest witchery beams,
  " And sparkles in her smile.
" In tranquil grace and beauty now
  " A matron in thy home
" Thou sitt'st ; but we, when spring-time comes,
  " As girls again will roam.
" Again we'll course along the meads,
  " And when our flowers we twine,
" Like lambs that for their mothers bleat,
  " Shall we for Helen pine.
" Then first for thee of melilot
  " We'll weave the votive wreath,
" And hang it up in Helen's name
  " Yon giant plane beneath.
" For thee from out the silver urn,
  " Where those broad branches spread,
" We'll draw our fragrant store, and there
  " The liquid perfume shed.
" On the smooth bark we'll grave the words,
  " That passers-by may see,
" In Doric phrase—' Oh ! harm me not—
  " ' For I am Helen's tree.'

ʺ Hail to the hero and his bride !—
 " And may Latona shower
ʺ (Fair offspring is Latona's gift)
 " Her blessings on your bower.
ʺ May she too in her might divine—
 " The Cyprian Goddess—give
ʺ That Love's pure flame in both your breasts
 " With equal ardour live.
" And Jove—great Jove—may he for aye
 " With wealth and honour grace
ʺ Sons after sires of noblest blood—
 " Your children's children's race.
ʺ Sleep, breathing confidence and joy !
 " Sleep on till day appear !
ʺ Forget not though to wake at dawn :
 " At dawn will we be here,
ʺ When the first feather'd songster's voice
 " Shall call us from our rest,
ʺ Till then farewell ! in Hymen's name
 " Be this fair wedding bless'd."

ON AN ANCIENT PANATHENAIC VASE IN A LONDON DRAWING-ROOM.

FROM the land of Attic song
    I was borne across the wave :
From the mirth of a festive throng,
    To the gloom of a Tuscan grave.

Where the harness on the dead
    Grew canker'd o'er with rust,
Where the hero on his bed
    Lay mouldering into dust.

And many an age and race
    Across broad Europe swept,
While in that narrow place
    My lonely watch I kept.

I reck'd not in my home,
  In the tomb beneath the sod,
Of the growth or fall of Rome,
  Or the change of Europe's God.

But empires wax'd and wan'd,
  And nations passed away,
While unbroken and unstain'd—
  Frail as I am—I lay.
        •

Still see upon my side
  The warrior-goddess stand :
How she poises in her stride
  Her lance with lifted hand.

As of yore in Homer's song,
  Unchang'd she seems to wield,
Terror of the Trojan throng,
  Her grisly Gorgon shield.

Now unheeding at her feet,
  All in silk and lace array'd,
Lisp and flirt and part and meet
  Flippant youth and fickle maid.

In a London Drawing-Room.

Grim and stiff she holds her place,
    Frowning from on high ;
Spectre of a creed and race,
    And of ages long gone by.

TRANSLATION OF COUNT PLATEN'S LINES, "DAS ENDE POLENS."

[Written on the occasion of a false report that Warsaw had been taken on the 28th of February (1831?) and Poland made a Russian province. The reader will recollect that the words "Finis Poloniæ" were said to be those uttered by Kosciusko when he fell wounded in the battle of Malikovicé in 1794, but were disclaimed by him in his letter to the Comte de Ségur.—See *Sutherland Edwards*, vol. i. p. 3.]

———•◇•———

I.

Ye noble hearts beneath the sod !
Grudge not the blood you've shed,
The time will come when pilgrim hands
Shall deck with flowers your bed :
The poet too will hither haste,
And sing in fearless strain

This hecatomb to liberty,
 Round Warsaw's ramparts slain ;
Nor shall your grave be hard to find
 By those who tread this ground,
A giant form—great Nemesis—
 Sits watching on its mound.

II.

What boots it that a thousand foes
 Have fall'n beneath your sword ?
The life-blood of a single Pole
 Is worth a Cossack horde :
And though the tyrant's slaves may lie,
 Here mingled in one grave,
With those who lavish'd all, and then
 Life for their country gave :
Fair Freedom's trophy on this spot
 Your country yet shall see,
And your Simonides shall sing
 This new Thermopylæ.

FREE TRANSLATION FROM THE ICE-LANDIC OF THE "EDDA."

"HELGAKVIDA HUNDINGSBANA," II., ST. 28.

"Trauðr em ek, systir!"

Lüning's "Edda," s. 339. Stanzas 37 and 49 are omitted.

THE first speaker is Hunding, the brother of Sigruna, who tells his sister that he has killed her husband, Helgi. Sigruna herself, her maiden or slave, the spirits of the dead, and Sigruna and Helgi in the grave, follow. Lüning and Simrock speak of this episode as containing the type of the story afterwards embodied in Bürger's "Lenore;" but in reality it is very different in character, and is far more striking and pathetic. The German poem, "Es stehen die Sterne am Himmel," of which the author is unknown, and which is printed in Bechstein's " Deutsches Lesebuch," s. 115 (if, as I suppose, it be genuine), really deprives Bürger of much of the credit given to him. The story is the same as in his " Lenore," but it is told with much greater simplicity. On the other hand, Sigruna resembles Lenore in nothing but the one fact, that each goes with her husband or her lover to the grave. Sigruna does this voluntarily, but the lady in both the other poems seems to be carried thither by main force, against her will. But there are other ballads which in this particular feature resemble the story of Sigruna more closely. In " William's Ghost " (Percy's " Relics," Ayton, ii., p. 98), we are told :—

> But she has kiltit her robes of green
> A piece below her knee,
> And a' the livelong winter's night
> The dead corpse follow'd she.

In the Danish ballad of "Aage and Else " (Grundtvig, B. ii. s. 493), the idea of the suffering inflicted on the dead lover by the sorrow of his living mistress is strongly expressed; and Grundtvig, no doubt rightly, derives this composition from the Icelandic original. He gives a spirited Danish version of the concluding stanzas here translated. " Clerk Saunders " is another Scotch ballad of a kindred character. " Aage and Else " will be found translated in Mr. Prior's *Danish Ballads* (vol. iii. p. 70), and the English reader will there see a prose version of a portion of the Icelandic story. Compare also Grimm, *Dänische Heldenlieder* (s. 73), and the *Fortnightly Review* (No. VI.) That the beauty and grandeur of the Icelandic are most inadequately reproduced in this translation or paraphrase, no one is more conscious than myself ; but the general train of thought and the feeling of the whole may perhaps in some degree be made accessible to the English reader. The two stanzas in ten-syllable metre represent the prose of Sæmund, connecting the verses with each other.

——◆◇◆——

1.

Hunding. Sister ! loth am I to show
The deed of death which works thee woe :
How Helgi, lov'd in bower and hall,
Before my sword was doom'd to fall :
That prince who in his royal seat
Trod necks of kings beneath his feet.

II.

Sigruna. May all the oaths thy friendship swore
Gnaw thy bosom to its core !
Sworn were they too by that dread stream
Where Leiptra's flashing waters gleam ;
Or by that rock that bathes its side
In the cool billow's swelling tide.

III.

May the ship that bears thee stay
Fetter'd on its watery way,
Even though the favouring gale
Come at call and fill her sail !
May the steed thou ridest stand
Restive to thy spur and hand,
Even though in battle strife
Foemen press thee for thy life !

IV.

May the sword thou wieldest fail
E'er to bite on shield or mail !
Never be its work well sped
Save when it sings around thy head !

Could I see thee, wolf-like, roam,
Reft of joy and wealth and home,
Snatching at some carrion food—
Then my vengeance were made good !

V.

Hunding. Wild and witless art thou grown,
Sister, thus to curse thine own.
Odin sow'd the seeds of hate,
Odin rules our bitter fate.
Take the half of all we hold,
Take the rings of good red gold,
Take Vigadale and Vandilsvê,
For thee and for thy sons to sway.

VI.

Sigruna. Within my bower at Snevafell
In sorrow night and day I dwell ;
Life is hateful to me, save
To spy that light o'er Helgi's grave
That heralds his return ;—at hand
Let his ready courser stand,
Golden-bitted Vigblær—then
I may clasp my lord again.

VII.

Ah ! my Helgi's sword of flame
All his foes had learn'd to tame,
Till beneath his wrathful eye
They and all their kin would fly,
As goats that, when the wolf is near,
Rush from the mountain, mad with fear.

VIII.

Tall and fair, my Helgi's form
Tower'd amid the warrior-swarm,
As some strong ash-tree on the heath   .
O'ershadows all the thorns beneath :
Or as that hart, the forest's pride,
With dewy flank and stately stride,
Moves 'mid the herd, and tosses high
His horns, that gleam against the sky.

IX.

Sigruna's maiden sat, and seem'd to mark
  How o'er the dreary heath there swept along,
With Helgi in their midst, at midnight dark,
  Toward the open grave, a ghostly throng.

X.

Sigruna's Ye shapes that passing by I see,
Maiden. Tell, O tell me, what ye be !
    Are ye phantoms of my brain ?
    Or are ye spirits of the slain,
    That spur the steed and shake the spear ?
    Is the end of all things here ?
    Or, as if by second birth,
    Are these warriors given to earth ?

XI.

Spirits. We are no phantoms of the brain :
    Spirits we of heroes slain,
    Spur the steed and shake the spear.
    The end of all things is not here ;
    Nor, as if by second birth,
    Are these warriors given to earth.

XII.

Maiden Sigruna ! list the tale I tell,
(to
Sigruna). And quit thy bower at Snevafell.
    Hie thee forth, my lady fair !
    The grave is open !—Helgi's there !

Hasten, if with eager grasp
It listeth thee thy lord to clasp.
Go, staunch the blood at his behest,
Welling from his wounded breast.

XIII.

Sigruna (in the tomb). That we two thus should meet again,
Helgi, makes thy wife as fain
As Odin's hawks that sniff afar
Fresh carnage on the field of war :
Or, bright with dew-drops, greet the day
That lights them to some new-slain prey.

XIV.

Let me kiss that brow so pale,
Ere we strip thee of thy mail ;
Let me clasp thee to my heart,
Stiff and bloody as thou art.
Thy matted hair is frosted o'er,
All thy limbs are smear'd with gore ;
Clammy are thy hands and brow—
My king ! how can I help thee now ?

XV.

Helgi. Thine eyes, my own Sigruna, shed
The dew of sorrow on this head.
When deck'd with gold, in beauty bright,
Thou weepest through the livelong night,
I feel each cruel tear-drop flow,
As cold and piercing, fraught with woe,
It trickles over Helgi's breast,
Benumbs his heart and breaks his rest.

XVI.

Nay—let us rather seek again
Affection's joyous cup to drain.
Gone are lands and life's bright morrow,
Yet will we chant no song of sorrow :
My bosom bleeds, but at my side
Sits in the grave my chosen bride.

XVII.

Sigruna. See, my Helgi, Ylfing's race
Here shall find fit resting-place ;
On this pillow lay thy head,
And let me smooth my hero's bed ;

For in the grave too I will rest
My loving cheek on Helgi's breast;
As when there beam'd a brighter day,
And by my living lord I lay.

XVIII.

Helgi. To sleep beneath this ghastly shade
Thou hast not fear'd, my royal maid!
But, warm in life and beauty's charms,
Hast clasp'd the dead within thine arms.
Högni's daughter! now I see
I may hope for all from thee;
Nor wilt thou still with tears and sighs
Vex the couch where Helgi lies.

XIX.

'Tis time for me to ride away,
Where the red streaks of dawning day
Have marked my path; there must I speed
O'er Bifröst's bridge my pallid steed;
And from my love must westward fly
Beyond the bow which spans the sky,
Before the cock wake with shrill call
The host within Valhalla's hall.

XX.

The warriors all were gone ; she sought her bower
 At Snevafell just as the morning broke ;
But by the grave again at midnight's hour
 She sat and watch'd for him, and thus she spoke :

XXI.

Sigruna.   Ah !—had he thought to come, I trow
     My warrior-king were with me now.
     From Valhalla Sigmund's son
     Long ere this his way had won.
     My hopes have wan'd.   The eagle's brood
     Have sought their perch in yonder wood ;
     And mortal men, save those who weep,
     Lie buried all in dreamy sleep.

THE VISIT OF THORFINN, EARL OF ORKNEY, TO KING MAGNUS.

A BALLAD SCENE.

I.

KING MAGNUS sate at his midday meal,
    Where his fleet at anchor rode,
When a stranger cross'd the royal deck,
    And straight to the table strode.

II.

He greeted the king ; he took the loaf
    That lay upon the board ;
And broke and ate, as if of right,
    Whilst neither spoke a word.

III.

King Magnus gaz'd ; as he wip'd his beard,
    " Wilt thou not drink ? " he said,
And pass'd the cup : the stranger drank,
    And bow'd in thanks his head.

IV.

" Thy name? "   " My name is Thorfinn, sir."
    " Earl Thorfinn can it be ? "
He smil'd—"Well, yes ; men call me thus
    " Beyond the western sea."

V.

" And is it so ? " the king replied ;
    " I had resolv'd me well,
" That if we two met——what passed when we met
    " Thou shouldst not live to tell.

VI.

" Together now we've broken bread
    " And thus my hand is stay'd ;
" But think thou not the score is quit,
    " Though vengeance be delay'd."

VII.

It chanced as friends they drank one day—
  On the deck a Norse-man stood :
" Lord earl," he said, " from thee I claim
  " The price of a brother's blood.

VIII.

" When Kirkwall-street was drench'd in gore,
  " And the king's men slaughter'd lay,
" By thy command that brother died—
  " Wilt thou his man-bote pay ? "

IX.

Loud laugh'd the earl—" What ho ! thou fool,
  " Thou must oft have heard it said,
" How Thorfinn scores of men hath slain,
  " But man-bote never paid."

X.

" All this, lord earl, is nought to me ;
  " 'Tis nought if our king sits by,
" Nor cares to avenge those men of his,
  " Led out like sheep to die."

XI.

Then Thorfinn look'd again, and swore,
　" By the rood, I know thee well—
" Why, I gave thee thy life in Kirkwall town,
　" When all thy comrades fell.

XII.

" My chance is hard—I have oft been blam'd
　" Too many that I slew,
" And now this coil hath come about
　" Because I have slain too few."

XIII.

The king's brow flushed with wrath : " Forsooth,
　" It seemeth to vex thee sore,
" That in thwarting my rights and slaying my men,
　" Thou hast not done still more."

XIV.

But now a fair breeze fills each sail,
　And pennons are floating free,
As the long war-ships, with their dragon heads,
　Go cleaving the dark blue sea.

XV.

And aye to the west of the Norway-fleet
Earl Thorfinn steers his bark ;
Men saw her holding her course with them
One night when the sky grew dark :

XVI.

But when morning broke that bark was gone
Far, far, o'er the western foam,
Where Orkney breasts the waves, and where
Earl Thorfinn sits in Kirkwall fair,
Sole lord of his island-home.

Note.—The incidents of this scene, if incidents they can be called, are to be found in the Orkney Saga ; and I may say that some of the very phrases of that prose narrative have been, as far as possible, faithfully imitated. Story, I am well aware, there is none, and the reader may ask as to the hero, " Que diable allait-il faire dans cette galère-là ? "

Thorfinn Earl of Orkney was the fourth son of Earl Sigurd, and survived his three elder brothers. After long feuds, he slew his nephew, Earl Rögnvald, the son of

Brusi, and put to death in cold blood the men of King Magnus, who had supported the claims of Rögnvald. This is the massacre at Kirkwall alluded to in the ballad.

Thorfinn held, not only the Orkneys, but also Caithness, and probably Galway and the Western Isles. He is said to have possessed nine earldoms in Scotland, and he was the ally of Macbeth, whose power, it has been conjectured, rested mainly on the influence of Thorfinn and the Norwegians of Orkney. That he plundered frequently in England and Ireland is a matter of course, and is duly recorded in the Saga. He died in 1064 A.D. The fleet which was assembled when Thorfinn paid his visit to King Magnus was intended to act against Denmark, and was commanded jointly by that king and by Harold, the son of Sigurd (Harðráði), who was subsequently killed at Stamfordbridge.—See *Munch, Chronicon Regum Manniæ*, pp. 48–50; *Orkneyinga Saga (Flateyjar Bok*, b. ii. s. 419).

London: Printed by SMITH, ELDER AND Co., Old Bailey, E.C.

www.ingramcontent.com/pod-product-compliance
Lightning Source LLC
Chambersburg PA
CBHW032044090426
42733CB00030B/657